Presented to

_____

from

_____

On this day

_____

You + Me

You + Me = Love

by Kelly Eileen Hake

A DayMaker Greeting Book

The smartest thing I ever did was *fall in love with you.*

I can't remember a single better idea than the one that brought us together.

You+ Me = Love

I love you

When I was a child I loved soaring through the air on a swing and believing I could touch the sky. . . . I haven't forgotten the thrill of those moments. . . and I experience anew that same kind of wonder and excitement *every time you hold my hand!*

S'ayapo
(Greek)

There is no more perfect way to start the day than spending time with you. Your smile fills the morning with warm comfort, and I love looking forward to more of the same tomorrow.

u o

(Latin)

No matter how many times or ways I tell you I love you, I'll never be able to express just how deeply I care for you.

For centuries men and women around the globe have loved one another.

Great works of art, song, and literature spring from this powerful emotion I

now share with you. Together, we can make our own loving legacy.

you are my dream ing dance oh love

May the Lord make your love increase and overflow for each other and for everyone

else. . . . *May he strengthen your hearts.*

1 THESSALONIANS 3:12–13

Je t'aime
(French)

Everything seems sweeter when you're with me. A serving of your smile or a shared moment of laughter is a precious gift I will never stop enjoying.

A l o h

w a u   i a ' o e
(Hawaiian)

You always know just
how to make each day a
celebration of us.

Wo ai ni
(Mandarin)

Whether it's an evening out on the town or at home playing board games,

I can't imagine life without you.

It doesn't matter what we do; so long as we're together it will be something

wonderful.

It's plain to see that knowing you has made me a better person. I don't mind if the whole world knows how special you make me feel *because you chose to love me.*

Ich liebe dich

(German)

$\mathcal{I}$ like to think that we're a lot
like music—sometimes lively and
fun, other times slow and serious,
occasionally flirty and loud, but
always in harmony with each other.

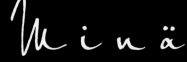

astan sinua

(Finnish)

Your small surprises,

Kind words,

Simple pleasures,

And thoughtful gestures

Always brighten my outlook!

Saya

(Malay)

When you smile, *I share your joy.*

When you are hurt, *I ache for you.*

When you laugh, *I delight in you.*

When you fail, *I lift you up.*

And when you look at me,

You will see *how deeply I love you.*

Thinking about you throughout our time apart is one of my better habits that I don't plan to break anytime soon.

Szeretlek

(Hungarian)

When I was small, I read all the fairy tales until I knew them by heart. When I grew older, I came to believe that such love could only be found between the pages of fiction. Now I know the truth behind the stories because you've given me my own happily-ever-after.

Travi

n i h y a a m i
(Sanskrit)

The love in your eyes
warms the coldest night, and
I melt a little whenever your
eyes meet mine.

Volim te

(Serbian)

I am always moved by how special you make me feel, as though you'd lay the world at my feet if you could.

The time we set aside from the hustle and bustle of every

day to enjoy each other are the high points of life.

Your love shines on me as we show

how much we care.

ras Liublu

(Russian)

Our love is ageless as the earth,

Strong and dependable as mountains,

Refreshing as the oceans,

Enduring as the sands of time.

ker dig
(Danish)

Valentine's Day is the only day when everyone celebrates love, but I know that each day with you is a celebration of the love we've found together.

Be mine forever!

Even after all the time we've spent together, I love how you still surprise me.

I love you

Our love will last a lifetime.

elska thig
(Icelandic)

Wherever you go,

you carry a piece of

my heart with you.

Tai m i

gra Leat

(Irish)

You have touched my heart in so many ways. When I look at you I know we grow stronger through even the slightest glance. I look forward to being with you until we're old and gray.

—Bryan Hobson

Te iubesc

(Romanian)

Since you've come into my life, I see things in a whole new light. When I glance at the stars *twinkling in the night sky,* I think of how bright you've made my world.

Whether you're singing along to your favorite song on the radio or whispering in my ear, *your voice is music to me!*

Amo-te

(Portuguese)

ISBN 1-59310-362-X

Designed by Julie Doll.

Published by Barbour Publishing, Inc., P.O. Box 719, Uhrichsville, Ohio 44683.
www.barbourbooks.com

*Our mission is to publish and distribute inspirational products
offering exceptional value and biblical encouragement to the masses.*

Printed in China.
5 4 3 2 1